ANISHINAABE WORLD NEWS

OJIBWE HISTORY, CULTURE, AND LANGUAGE

CONTENTS

ANISHINAABE WORLDVIEWS
OJIBWE HISTORY, CULTURE, AND LANGUAGE

The family, the roles played by family members, the functions of the family, the customs surrounding family life and the spiritual dimension of family are the center of American Indian culture.

INDINAWE MAAGANAG: "ALL MY RELATIVES"

Traditional American Indian *(Anishinaabe)* families include a wide circle of relatives who are linked together in mutual dependence. Family members share resources and responsibilities. The encompassing concept of family is referred to as an extended family. There is also a spiritual dimension to the idea of family. The Dakota use the phrase *mita-kuyapi-owasin* which means all my relatives. All my relatives includes not only the Dakota, but all human life, plant life, animal life and all things of this Earth. The Ojibwe used the term *indinawe maaganag* which can also be translated *all my relatives.*

American Indians use the symbol of a *circle* to describe the kinship and interrelationship of all of nature. The family is a circle with each member playing a reciprocal role. The life passages through which we all move are a circle. The seasons of the year form a circle.

Since the appearance of the Europeans on the American continent, American Indians have been struggling to retain the right to freedom, land, tradition and a way of life, that is, for Indian values. This struggle for *cultural survival* has never been easy – not during the days of *colonization* nor today during economic competition and culture clash. The majority of American Indians were forced to live in poverty during the past 300 years.

Poverty is corrosive and destructive to *culture* and the *values* embedded in the culture. The well-known results of poverty are family disintegration which causes further deterioration in the social structure and the social fiber. Social fiber is based upon a *shared value system* in which individual and group attitudes are shaped. Norms for behavior often represent cultural ideals and are not necessarily observed on a daily basis. It is a primary interest of parents to equip their children with the tools of survival. The survival of the children and the survival of the culture are related.

EXTENDED FAMILY

American Indian families include a wide circle of relatives who share resources and responsibilities. Family includes more than parents and children. Families include grandparents, uncles and aunts, cousins and many others. This wider concept of family is called an extended family.

The circle of relatives who live together or in close proximity are linked in *mutual dependence*. Grandparents and other community elders have always played a major role in rearing and educating the young. It is customary in many tribes for the grandparents to raise one or more of their grandchildren. This type of shared responsibility for parenting is a family and community strength. The grandchild is an extension of the grandmother and grandfather.

ANISHINAABE

In the Ojibwe language there are kinship terms for children and other family members. In the Anishinaabe kinship system, younger siblings are not distinguished by gender. They are called *Nii-she-may*, my younger sibling. Older brother is called *Nii-sa-yay* and older sister, *Nii-mi-say.* Aunts and uncles are distinguished according to whether these aunts and uncles are related through the mother's or father's side of the family. Maternal uncle, for example, is called *Niizhi-shay*, and paternal uncle, *Nii-mee-shu-may.* Great grandchildren are called *Inda-ni-kubi-ji-gan*, which literally means two pieces of rope spliced together or "what I have spliced."

Many Anishinaabe children have more than one personal name given at different times. Children may receive one or more names when they are small. An elder may give a child their name. Parents customarily bring tobacco to the elder who they want to name their child. The name comes to the elder in a dream. The parents then prepare a ceremonial feast. After receiving a name, the child and elder are bonded in a special relationship. They call each other, *nii-ya-wé e* meaning my namesake.

A child may be given a nickname rendered either in Ojibwe or English. This name reveals something about the child's special character.

Examples of naming occasions:
Birth name
Formal name
Nickname
Name given during illness
Name given at puberty – named after one of personal attributes
A child's name may be that of an elder who has passed on.

Family refers to a wide circle of relatives who belong to the same *clan*. A clan is symbolized as a species of bird, animal or fish. There are many bands or divisions of the Anishinaabe nation. Within this large nation are 20 or more clans.

One definition of family is the Ojibwe word *in-do-daim* meaning my clan. Those who belong to the same clan consider one another close relatives. In the past as well as today, children are cared for by a circle of relatives. Grandparents, aunts and uncles, and fathers as well as mothers take responsibility. Anishinaabe child rearing includes the conviction that harsh discipline destroys the child's spirit. Positive discipline takes place through adult example, encouragement and community recognition of the child's accomplishments,

FAMILY DEVELOPMENT

Parenting encompasses the following time periods, beginning at birth:

Infancy (birth to two years),
Early Childhood (two to six years),
Middle Childhood (six to twelve years)
and Adolescence (puberty to adulthood).

During these time periods children develop in the following major areas: *physical, cognitive (thinking abilities), social and emotional*; and what is called moral development or *moral reasoning* including *spiritual development.*

Parents change and continue to develop as well. In come cases parenthood begins in adolescence. Parents develop through early and middle adulthood to late adulthood and older, possibly in the role of grandparents. Each developmental stage has its specific tasks that need to be accomplished and certain goals to be achieved. Also, each major stage has its difficult transitions, hurdles and sometimes, it's crises. For the parenting adult there is a transition into responsible adulthood, a mid-life transition and an adjustment to late adult life.

American Indian tribes and individuals mark the passages of life through ceremony, ritual and prayer. There are special ceremonies and practices at birth, naming, puberty and marriage. When a person moves back to the spirit world, the passing is marked by ritual and ceremony. Teachers should be aware that American Indian families may or may not continue to practice in the traditional ways.

FAMILY, GENDER ROLES AND RESPONSIBILITIES

In the old ways, *gender and family roles* and responsibilities were clear. One of the most important philosophical beliefs in this area is that of *equality*. While gender roles and responsibilities were and are clear, the concept of equality is paramount.

Women have traditionally been responsible for the home and *men* have been the providers and protectors. It is not unheard of for role reversal to occur and when it does occur the community does not condemn such behavior. Both men and women have been and are warriors, hunters, teachers, medicine people and leaders who offer their gifts to the community.

Basil Johnston, author of many books about Ojibwe life and culture, speaks about this concept of equality, both in relationships between men and women and in the role of children in the family. "The Anishinaabe word for the relationship between a man and a woman was *"weekjeewaugun,"* meaning companion – a term which referred equally to male or female. There was no distinction in sex; no notion of inferiority or superiority. More particularly, weedjeewaugun meant Companion on the Path of Life – *"he who goes with"* or *"she who walks with."*

For both men and women, a companion was someone to walk with and be with through all aspects of life and living. Such was the notion of marriage; the taking of a companion. It was the strongest of bonds. In describing the role of children, Mr. Johnston says,

"A woman may give birth to many children. To all she gives food, care, and a place near her. To each she gives a portion of herself; to each she assigns a place in the household. No child by virtue of priority of birth or other attributes may demand for him or herself more than the brothers or sisters. A mother gives equally to all of her

children, from first to last, from strong to weak. All are entitled to a place near her bosom, her lodge. Her gift does not diminish but increases and renews itself."

THE COMMUNITY WAY OF TEACHING A CHILD

Traditional American Indian approaches to *teaching* and *learning* provide a powerful model for a constructive learning environment. Learning in the community was and is vastly different from what usually happens in a formal classroom. In these next two paragraphs, *Jane Deborah Wyatt* provides a description of the contrast. [1]

"In the community, the usual way for a child to learn a skill from an adult is to observe carefully over long periods of time and then to begin taking part in the activity. The way in which a native child learns the technology of fishing is a good example. By accompanying adults on fishing trips and by listening and observing, a child learns places for fishing and how to set nets, use a dip net, and prepare the fish for eating. A child also learns names of different types of fish, parts of the fish, types of nets and assorted gear, and styles of preparation. All of this is learned by watching and doing with a minimum of verbal preparation or interchange.

Similarly it would be unusual for an adult to ask a child to verbalize what has been learned; whether or not the child had taken in and retained the information would be evident in the next fishing trip. A child may of course, ask questions about the skills being performed, and the adult may supplement the actual performance with verbal commentary. However, verbal instructions without demonstration and participation, a frequent occurrence in the schools, are rare in the community."

Storytelling in a community setting is also quite different. During a fishing trip a story about other trips or about the history of the area might be told, or the same information might be told weeks later in a totally different context. In either case, once the story was started, it might continue for hours. It would be considered stifling to limit a storyteller to twenty-minute sessions. Yet this is precisely what is done in school. During storytelling sessions in the community children are expected to listen quietly. At the end no one asks them to recite the names of the main characters or to answer questions about plot, motivation and moral. In the school classroom the essence of learning is the articulation of information and skills in verbal and written form according to a predetermined timetable, and quizzing to determine if students have retained information."

Wyatt, June Deborah. "Native Involvement in Curriculum Development: The Native American Teacher as Cultural Broker," Interchange, 9, No. 1, 1978-79.

ROLE OF ELDERS

Elders have a very special place in the community and in the family. According to *Basil Johnston*, in <u>*Ojibwe Heritage*</u>,

"It was the elders, grandmothers and grandfathers, who taught about life, through stories, parables, fables, allegories, songs, chants and dances. They were the ones who had lived long enough and had had a path to follow, and were deemed to possess the qualities for teaching wisdom, knowledge, patience and generosity."

Grandmothers teach young women their roles and responsibilities. Grandfathers teach the young men. Grandmother or *Nokomis* has a special place in the teachings and stories of the Anishinabe people.

Most of the stories begin with Nokomis and her grandson. Nokomis raised her grandson, who is **Waynaboshoo/Winnebozhoo/Nanabozho*.

It is not unusual today for grandparents to continue to raise grandchildren. It is also traditional for aunts and uncles to help with the discipline of the children.

EFFECTS OF GOVERNMENT ASSIMILATION POLICIES

The assimilation policies of the federal government were purposeful and part of a systematic effort to remove the *traditional values, languages, history and culture* from American Indians. These policies had and continue to have a tremendous detrimental effect on American Indian culture and language.

Some of these policies include: creating a *reservation* system making a *relocation policy* (government efforts to transfer American Indians from reservations to urban centers) instituting an *allotment policy* to break up the American Indian land base sending young American Indian children to federal and mission *boarding schools*

Many of the children sent to boarding schools were not allowed to go home except for periodic visits. In these schools, the history of American Indian tribes was not included in the American story, with pre-contact history treated with a few paragraphs in most texts. Children in boarding schools seldom learned the *oral history* of their tribes from their elders and storytellers. This had a serious effect on the self-worth and self-esteem of American Indian children. Many of them had a sense of alienation from the political, social and economic makeup of the country. Unfortunately, this practice of exclusion continues today in many history texts and schools.

Public school education may have a similarly negative impact when not inclusive of an American Indian worldview. *Note: Different spellings are used by people in different areas. With the implementation of the federal policy of sending young children to federal and mission boarding schools, a link between the elders and the young was broken. Children came back from these schools unable to speak their traditional languages with any degree of sophistication.

In many cases, they had been led to believe the language should not be spoken at all. As the children of these schools became adults, many chose to not teach their traditional language and culture to their children. Their own memories of the punishment for speaking their language at these schools was much too painful. Many had been put into isolation and beaten for doing it and the only future they saw for their own children was to completely *assimilate* into the American way of life. This is a common element of many invaded groups (Freire, 1973):

"For cultural invasion to succeed, it is essential that those invaded become convinced of their intrinsic inferiority. Since everything has its opposite, if those who are invaded considered themselves inferior, they must necessarily recognize the superiority of the invaders. The values of the latter become the pattern of the former. The more invasion is

accentuated and those invaded are alienated from the spirit of their own culture and from themselves, the more the latter want to be like the invaders; to walk like them, dress like them, talk like them."

It should be noted that some individuals had *positive experiences* in these schools and can relate instances of friendships formed, skills learned, and needs for food, clothing and shelter met. The policy of assimilation also affected some American Indians' views about leadership.

In the past, the tribal community may have been able to draw upon the perceived wisdom of elders and other persons of knowledge. With the decline in the number of elders who practice traditional lifestyles and beliefs, the decline in respect for tradition, and the encroachment of leadership styles based upon political power, many reservation communities saw a decline in the number of traditional leaders.

In many boarding schools, boys were trained to be farmers and girls to be homemakers. With this process of *Americanization*, they were implicitly taught that men and women were not equal. This conflicted with traditional ways. Before the coming of the European immigrants to this land, women were considered the equals of men among the Anishinaabe.

The policy of assimilation did not wane until well into the 20th century. Until recently, social service authorities often placed American Indian children in need of such services into Euro-American foster homes. *The Indian Child Welfare Act* finally set guidelines whereby if American Indian children were removed from their homes, every effort had to be made to place them in American Indian homes.

THE AMERICAN INDIAN FAMILY TODAY

In the American Indian family today, parents continue to teach children in the old ways. Many parents expose their children to *traditional storytellers* whenever possible and make efforts to tell the old stories. The traditional behavior management techniques are still in use in many families, albeit not as effective when young people are bombarded from all sides by the media, materialism, and social issues like racism, poverty and chemical dependency.

While most American Indian infants are no longer carried in cradleboards, parents understand the need to be close to infants and to provide nurturance to them. Many American Indian families understand the need to maintain harmony and balance in the home and to be at one with the environment.

STUDENT READINGS:

LAWS OF THE LODGE
Teachings of Wabasha (Also ascribed to Tecumseh, Sitting Bull, Crazy Horse and Wovoka)

Be hospitable.

Be kind.

Always assume that your guest is tired, cold and hungry. Even if a hungry dog enters your lodge, you must feed him.

Always give your guest the place of honor in the lodge, and at the feast, and serve him in reasonable ways.

Never sit while your guest stands.

Go hungry rather than stint your guest. If he refuses certain food, say nothing, he may be under a vow.

Protect your guest as one of the family and feed his horse.

Do not trouble your guest with many questions about himself, he will tell you what he wishes you to know.

In another person's lodge, follow their customs, not your own.

Never worry your host with your troubles.

Always repay calls of courtesy; do not delay.

Give your host a little present on leaving; little presents are little courtesies and never give offense.

Say, "Thank you" for every gift, however small.

Compliment your host, even if you must strain the facts to do so.

Never come between anyone and the fire.

Never walk between persons talking. Never interrupt persons talking.

In council, listen attentively to the other person's words as though they were words of wisdom, however much they may be otherwise.

Let not the young speak among those much older, unless asked.

Always give a place to your seniors in entering or leaving the lodge. Never sit while your seniors stand.

Never force your conversation on anyone.

Let silence be your motto till duty bids you speak. Speak softly, especially before your elders or in the presence of strangers.

Do not touch live coals with a steel knife or any sharp steel.

Do not break a marrowbone in the lodge; it is unlucky.

The women of the lodge are the keepers of the fire, but the men should help with the heavier sticks.

When setting up the tepees, keep the camp circle with its opening to the east, the door of each teepee to the sunrise.

Let each teepee be in its place, as long ago appointed by the old men – the wise ones – the night kin near other, and the clans of different totems facing across the circle.
In this way the young men shall see that they must marry across the circle of the camp, never with their close kin in the nearer lodges.

Adapted from "BEINGS FROM ANOTHER WORLD"
Leo J. Ambrose

Will people from Mars ever invade and conquer our planet? Probably not, but it they did, it might teach us how American Indians felt as they saw the people from Europe, in the course of a few centuries, take over North America.

In Minnesota, it might help us to understand how desperate Dakota Indians felt a century ago, when they suddenly turned against the settlers, killing many of them and destroying their property.

What caused the *Sioux Uprising of 1862*? Although separate incidents combined to bring about that tragedy, yet behind it all lay the long history of the white man's invasion of the American Indians' homeland. Let us consider how we might act under similar conditions.

Suppose our earth were invaded by Martians or other beings from outer space who, upon their arrival, destroy our newspapers, radio stations, telephone systems, and all other means of communication. Then they begin systematically to occupy our country. We hear rumors of what is going on in other parts of the land, but the invasion does not become a reality to us until, some morning, a group of Martians appears at our door and demands entry.

They walk into our living room and order us to pack our belongings. Then we are to stand ready for a vehicle to pick us up and take us away. Naturally we would protest. We would say, "This is our home! We own it! You have no right to put us out in this way!"

But the space beings would answer calmly, "This is all perfectly legal. We signed a treaty last month with the governor of Wisconsin. And under the terms of that treaty, all the land from Chicago to Fargo, North Dakota, and from Canada to the Iowa border now belongs to us. We need that region. It has natural resources that you have never discovered and are too ignorant to use."

"However, we are civilized and kindly beings. We're not going to throw you out to shift for yourselves. We have provided a spot for you in eastern Montana, where we will take you. There you will be allowed to make another home and start life over again. Besides this, we'll help you. We'll send experts to advise you on how to build houses in the Martian style, and dietitians who will teach you how to raise and prepare food in the Martian manner. We will send missionaries to show you the error of your present religious beliefs, and once a year we will send each family $200 worth of packaged foods and $50 in cash, to pay for the land we are taking."

Possibly we would obey the orders meekly and allow ourselves to be taken out to the western plains, though it is doubtful that we would. But let us assume that we take the Martians at their word. We move out to Montana and "begin life anew". Because the invaders have destroyed our economy, we have little choice but to cooperate with them.

We try to live as Martians, even though we do not like their way of life and do not feel comfortable in their strange houses. But we make every effort to exist under the conditions that are prescribed, although we hate it and are often hungry. Let us assume that we succeed partially. Then, just as we are beginning to feel that life is possible under those conditions, another group of Martians arrives and builds a trading center nearby.

This seems at first like a fine thing, for many items are sold there which we need in order to live. But in time we find that some of the articles, which look so attractive, turn out to be worthless trash. Worst of all, some of them are very harmful, but we do not find this out until it is too late.

Since we have no money, the traders offer to let us have these articles on credit. But the Martians have a business system, which we do not understand, and when the time arrives for our promised cash, we find that we owe the entire sum to the traders. So we are still penniless and hungry. Don't you think that we would more and more resent the situation, which our guardians have set up for us? But perhaps in desperation we still try to cooperate in order to survive.

Then, a few months later, a group of Martian officials descend on our little colony, announcing, "When we settled you here, we promised that you might stay forever, but since that time conditions have changed. We're sorry, but now we need this land. However, we have signed a treaty with the mayor of Sioux City, Iowa, and under the provisions of that treaty, you are now to move to a beautiful spot in the desert farther west. You will be just as well taken care of there as you were here. And we guarantee that this time we will really observe every condition of the treaty."

Finally we would feel, in desperation, that we could no longer endure such treatment. We would feel that it was better to die trying to throw off our oppressors than to continue such a life. We might be ready to cry out with Patrick Henry: "Give me liberty or give me death!" This story is only a fantasy, for we have not been attacked by beings from another world. But for American Indians, this really happened.

Their homeland was really taken away. In the process, they were treated in an unbelievably cruel manner, and almost every promise made was violated. American Indians, who are as proud of their ancestry and way of life as other groups are of theirs, were again and again subjected to unspeakable indignities, against which they had no defense.

They were tricked, cheated, robbed, and even murdered. In fact, the incidents described in our fantasy of the Martians would seem mild in comparison with what happened to American Indians of Minnesota less than a century ago.

The material in this article is taken from an address given by Mr. Ambrose before a Civil and Sioux War Conference sponsored by the Twin Cities Civil War Round Table and the Minnesota Historical Society. The Article was printed in the Gopher Historian for Fall 1962.

LIFE AT THE BOARDING SCHOOLS
Keith L. Pearson Social Studies Skills for Indian Adults
United Tribes Educational Technical Center Bismarck, North Dakota

"The boarding school environment was based on the conviction that Indian traditions were useless. The Indian Bureau directed its agents to take Indian children from their parents "first by persuasion; if this fails, then by withholding rations or annuities or by other such means as may reach the desired end.""

In other words, it made no difference whether the parents agreed or not to part with their children. At the boarding schools, children were forbidden to use any language but English. If they did not know how to speak English, they had to remain silent until they learned. They had to attend classes and worship services and clothing was often flimsy or ragged, and the diet was generally lacking to do heavy work on the schools' farms and in their laundries, boiler rooms, and offices.

The children were not permitted to return to their families until they had completed schooling, even if this took several years. During vacations the children either remained at the school or were taken home by missionary families or other volunteers. As far as the federal government was concerned, the boarding school program was an unqualified success. During the 1880's Congress approved funds for the construction of additional boarding schools in the reservation themselves. Fences were build around the reservations schools to separate the students from the reservation Indians, and to keep the children from running away."

What Was School Like?
Barney Drouillard, Grand Portage Enrollee, Grand Portage, Minnesota

"I have to give my mother credit for not having to send all of us kids to boarding school. …Us older kids, we had to go; my mother had a tough time with money, she was taking care of everything…That Catholic boarding school was hard. The work was hard, we wore the old raggy clothes that churches sent us.

We were sick a lot. I'll never forget that one boy died of pneumonia. He was sleeping out on a porch away from the rest of us because he was being punished for something, and it was cold, and he'd been sick too. It was terrible…After a while we went to the government boarding school…

That school was better. We had nicer clothes, you know, good quality clothes…and food was good, and the work wasn't so hard. We always thought our two youngest brothers were lucky, though. They got to stay with our mother go to school at home. We miss our mother."

--From A Childhood in Minnesota by Helen L. Carlson, Linda LeGarde Grover and Daniel W. Anderson with the assistance of Bonnie A. Cusick.

Indian Boarding School Multi-Generational Cycle

By Julene Kennerly

Education Specialist Gonzaga University, Spokane, Washington

"The endeavor to educate the Native American Indian into the English civilization had been as tedious and frustrating to the White culture as it was to the Indians. Communication barriers contributed to the ill-fated attempt to allow the Indian to fully accept and understand the English education system. The Joseph Study, published in 1969, cited problems: the lack of knowledge, vision, historical perspective, understanding of the Indian experience and the inability to listen to or accept Indian recommendations for change.

English education was contrary to the traditional oral modes of education of Indians. Indian education consisted of training youth by prayer, storytelling, memory skills, and listening. As the intrusion process swept across North America, the traditional education format of the Indians was interrupted, however it remains within us to this day. The missionary movement to educate the Indians, by establishing mission boarding schools on or near Indian reservations, was one of the primary attempts that affected me directly.

I am a third generation of mission and U.S. Government boarding schools. My grandfather obtained his English education at a Catholic mission, as did my father. My mother attended an out of state Indian boarding school. I grew up in a crowded home in the country on the Blackfeet Indian Nation. Even though my parents did not practice traditional Blackfeet ways, the values remained in our home.

My parents were proud Indians, who refused to take charity and taught their children to do the same. Our home was clean and so were the people who occupied it. We were taught to respect others and ourselves. Our elders had a special role within our society as teachers.

One of my fondest memories is of my grandfather sitting at the old round wooden table surrounded by his grandchildren, telling us a story by the light of the kerosene lamp. The story always contained a valuable lesson. Isolation from any public education facility was the criteria for me attending the Government boarding school.

The United States Government mandated that all Indian children had to attend school. My parents had no choice or they would be penalized with a sentence in jail until I did. History tells of the older generation being rounded up by bounty men and delivered to the doorsteps of the missions and boarding schools at which time they received their bounty.

My first day at the boarding school, my mom had a stream of tears flowing down her cheeks as she said good-bye to her little six-year-old. She knew she would not see her again until Christmas, that is, if they had transportation and the weather permitted them to make the fifty-mile trip. I was a confused, bewildered little girl who had never been away from home before and I didn't know what to expect. I wondered why I had to stay there and kept asking, "Why couldn't I go home with my parents?"

No one would answer me. That was the beginning of many unanswered questions and the origin of a little girl who soon learned that she did everything wrong. She felt she was a very bad person and unworthy of this earth. "Why would they be doing this to me if I was okay?"

The warmth of my parent's hugs had barely cooled when I begin to experience my English education. My hair was cut and kerosene was poured over it. The oil smelt awful. After that I was put under a shower, I had never seen a shower before and I remember screaming and crying. My skin was scrubbed until it was red and then a liquid poured over it that made it sting.

I remember sleeping in a bed alone (I had never experienced that before) between cold white sheets and I was scared and my heart hurt. That was the first time I ever remember having an actual heartache. I wanted to be home so much. I cried all night, but silently, after the matron heard me and said, "If you want to cry, I'll give you something to cry for."

The next morning at breakfast, I was served mush that was lumpy and had black things in it. I couldn't eat it, but I had to sit until I did. I stuffed it in my pocket. When the matron saw what I had done, I was made to kneel on a broomstick with my hands in the air. Although the intention of my presence at the boarding school was to be educated, I don't remember a teacher or a classroom. My memory blocks them out.

It seemed important to the school personnel that I learn to live the English lifestyle rather than learning academics. I remained at the boarding school until a little country school one mile from our home opened. Although my educational experience was tragic, there has been a tremendous attempt to rectify and improve the techniques of Indian education.

My boarding school experiences were not all hurtful. I believe the discipline assisted me to encounter life's challenges. Many residential boarders were grateful for the sanction of them. It was preferred over their home environment, be it because of food, shelter or family situations.

I am what life has shared with me. I will be what life will share with me. May it be I can pass on to others in empathy."

OJIBWEMOWIN

BASIC OJIBWE WORDS AND PHRASES

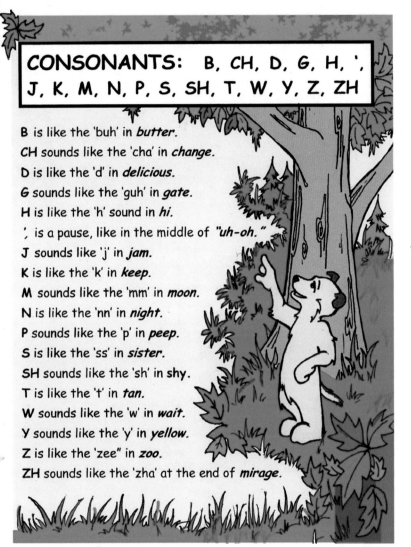

CONSONANTS: B, CH, D, G, H, ',
J, K, M, N, P, S, SH, T, W, Y, Z, ZH

B is like the 'buh' in *butter*.
CH sounds like the 'cha' in *change*.
D is like the 'd' in *delicious*.
G sounds like the 'guh' in *gate*.
H is like the 'h' sound in *hi*.
' is a pause, like in the middle of *"uh-oh."*
J sounds like 'j' in *jam*.
K is like the 'k' in *keep*.
M sounds like the 'mm' in *moon*.
N is like the 'nn' in *night*.
P sounds like the 'p' in *peep*.
S is like the 'ss' in *sister*.
SH sounds like the 'sh' in *shy*.
T is like the 't' in *tan*.
W sounds like the 'w' in *wait*.
Y sounds like the 'y' in *yellow*.
Z is like the 'zee" in *zoo*.
ZH sounds like the 'zha' at the end of *mirage*.

DOUBLE VOWEL CHART
This is how to pronounce Ojibwe words.

"Zh"- sounds like the "su" in
measure
"a"- sounds like the "u" in *sun*
"aa"- sounds like the "a" in *father*
"i"- sounds like the "i" in *sit*
"ii"- sounds like the "ee" in *feet*
"o"- sounds like the "o" in *go*
"oo"- sounds like the "oo" in *food*
"e"- sounds like the "ay" in *stay*

GREETINGS AND FEELINGS

Boozhoo - "Hello"

Aaniin - "Hi, How are you? How are things?"

Nimino-ayaa - "I'm well, I'm fine."

Giin dash? - "And you."

Miigwech - "Thank you."

Giga-waabamin minawaa - "I'll see you again."

Giga-waabamin naagaj - "See you later"

Giga-waabamininim minawaa - "I'll see you people again."

Nii - "I, me"

Gii - "You"

Nishkaadizi - "S/he is angry."

Menwendam - "S/he is happy."

Bakade - "S/he is hungry.

Maanendam - "S/he is sad"

Aakozi - "S/he is sick."

Mino-giizigad - "It is a good day."

Gimiwan - "It is raining."

Zoogipon - "It is snowing."

Noodin - "It is windy."

Gizhide - "It is hot."

Gisinaa - "It is cold."

Waaseyaa - "It is sunny."

Ningwaakod - "It is cloudy."

Gichi - "Great"

Manidoo - "Spirit"

WEATHER

Mino-giizhigad - It is a good day.

Mino-giizhigan - It is a good day.

Gimiwan - It is raining.

Gichi-gimiwan - It is raining hard.

Zoogipon - It is snowing.

Gichi-zoogipon - It is snowing hard.

Noodin - It is windy.

Gichi-noodin - It is very windy.

Gizhide - It is hot.

Gichi-gizhide - It is very hot.

Gisinaa - It is cold.

Gichi-gisinaa - It is very cold.

Zaagaate - It is sunny.

Gichi-zaagaate - It is very sunny.

Ningwaakod - It is cloudy.

Gichi-ningwaakod - It is very cloudy.

It is·

A cool wind- **Dakaasin**

Clear- **Mizhakwad**

Cloudy- **Ningwaanakwad**

Foggy- **Awan**

It Freezes Over(lake)- **Gashkadin**

Nasty Weather- **Niiskaadad**

Slippery- **Ozhaashaa**

There are Northern Lights- **Waawaate**

There is a tornado or whilrwind- **Ashibishidosh**

Thundering- **Animikiikaa**

Warm and mild- **Aabawaa**

Windy- **Noodin**

QUESTIONS, PHRASES AND EMOTIONS

Do you remember?- *Gimikwenden ina?*

How are you?- *Aaniin ezhi-ayaayan?*

How is it outside(what is the weather like)?- *Aaniin ezhiwebak agwajiing?*

How old are you?- *Aaniin endaso-biboonagiziyan?*

What are you called(name)?- *Aaniin ezhinikaazoyan?*

Where are you from?- *Aandi wenjibaayan?*

Where are you going?- *Aandi ezhaayan?*

Come here!- *Ondaas*

Come in- *Bendigen*

Hurry up - *Wewiib*

Wait - *Wait*

Please- *Daga*

Say it again(repeat)- *Ikidon miinawaa*

I am...

Afraid- Ningotaaj

Cold- Ningiikaj

Crazy- Ningiiwanaadiz

Hungry- Nimbakade

Mad- Ninishkaadiz

Resting- Nindanweb

Sad- Ningashkendam

Sick- Nindaakoz

Sorry- Nimaanendam

Thirsty- Ninoondeminikwe

Tired- Nindayekoz

Warm- Ningiizhooz

Well- Nimino-ayaa

Working- Nindanokii

ANIMALS

Ant(s)- Enigoons(ag)

Bass(s)- Ashigan(ag)

Bear(s)- Makwa(g)

Beaver(s)- Amik(wag)

Bee(s)- Aamoo(g)

Bird(s)- Bineshii(yag)

Blackbird(s)- Asiginaak(wag)

Bluejay(s)- Diindiisi(wag)

Bobcat(s)- Gidagaa-bizhiw(ag)

Butterfly(s)- Memengwaa(g)

Buffalo(s)- Mashkodebizhiki(wag)

Cat(s)- Gaazhagens(ag)

Chickadee(s)- Gijigaaneshii(yag)

Chicken(s)- Baaka' aakwe(yag)

Chipmunk(s)- Agongosens(ag)

Coyote(s)- Wiisagi-ma' iingan(ag)

Cow(s)- Bizhiki(wag)

Crane(s)- Mooshka' oosi(wag)

Crow(s)- Aandeg(wag)

Deer(s)- Waawaashkeshi(wag)

Dog(s)- Animosh(ag)

Dragonfly(ies)- Boochikwanishi(wag)

Duck(s)- Zhiishiib(ag)

Bald Eagle(s)- Migizi(wag)

Golden Eagle(s)- Giniw(ag)

Firefly(ies)- Waawaatesi(wag)

Fish(s)- Giigoo(yag)

Fly(ies)- Ojiins(ag)

Fox(es)- Waagosh(ag)

Frog(s)- Omakakii(g)

Canadian Goose(geese)- Nika(g)

Snow Goose(geese)- Wewe(g)

Hawk(s)- Gekek(wag)

Horse(s)- Bebezhigooganzhii(g)

Hummingbird(s)- Nenookaasi(wag)

Loon(s)- Maang(wag)

Mallard(s)- Aninshib(ag)

Marten(s)- Waabizheshi(wag)

Mink(s)- Zhaangweshi(wag)

Minnow(s)- Giigoozens(ag)

Moose(s)- Mooz(oog)

Mosquito(s)- Zagime(g)

Mouse(mice)- Waawaabigonoojii(yag)

Muskrat(s)- Wazhashk(wag)

Northern Pike(s)- Ginoozhe(g)

Oriole(s)- Asiginaak(wag)

Owl(s)- Gookooko' oo(g)

Otter(s)- Nigig(wag)

Partridge(s)- Bine(wag)

Pheasant(s)- Mayagi-bine(wag)

Pig(s)- Gookoosh(ag)

Porcupine(s)- Gaag(wag)

Rabbit(s)- Waabooz(oog)

Raccoon(s)- Esiban(ag)

Robin(s)- Opichi(wag)

Skunk(s)- Zhigaag(wag)

Sparrow(s)- Gakaashkinejii(wag)

Spider(s)- Asabikeshii(yag)

Squirrel(s)- Ajidamoo(g)

Snake(s)- Ginebig(oog)

Painted turtle(s)- Miskwaadesi(wag)

Snapping turtle(s)- Mikinaak(wag)

Sturgeon(s)- Name(wag)

Sucker(s)- Namebin(ag)

Sunfish(s)- Agwadaashi(wag)

Thunderbird(s)- Binesi(wag)

Turkey(s)- Mizise(g)

Turtle(s)- Mishiike(yag)

Vulture(s)- Wiinaange(wag)

Walleye(s)- Ogaa(wag)

Weasel(s)- Zhingos(ag)

Whitefish(s)- Adikameg(wag)

Wolf(wolves)- Ma' iingan(ag)

Woodchuck(s)- Makakojiishi(wag)

Downey Woodpecker(s)- Baapaase(wag)

Pileated Woodpecker(s)- Meme(g)

Woodtick(s)- Ezigaa(g)

Wren(s)- Anaamisagadaweshii(wag)

NUMBERS

One- **Bizhig**

Two- **Niizh**

Three- **Niswi**

Four- **Niiwin**

Five- **Naanan**

Six- **Ningodwaaswi**

Seven- **Niizhwaaswi**

Eight- **Nishwaaswi**

Nine- **Zhaangaswi**

Ten- **Midaaswi**

Eleven to nineteen add Ashi before number

Eleven- Ashi bezhig

Twenty to twenty-nine add **Niizhtana** ashi before number

Twenty-one- Niizhtana ashi bezhig

Thirty to thirty-nine add **Nisimidana ashi**

Thirty-one- Nisimidana ashi bezhig

Forties add **Niimidana** ashi

Forty-one- Niimidana ashi bezhig

Fifties add **Naanimidana** ashi

Fifty-one- Naanimidana ashi bezhig

Sixties add **Ningodwaasimidana** ashi

Seventies add **Niizhwaasimidana** ashi

Eighties add **Nishwaasimidana** ashi

Nineties add **Zhaangasimidana** ashi

Hundreds add **Ningodwaak** ashi

MONTHS

January(Great Spirit Moon)- **Gichi-Manidoo-Giizis**

February(Sucker Fish Moon)- **Namebini-Giizis**

March(Crust on the Snow Moon)- **Onaabani-Giizis**

April(Sap Boiling Moon)- **Iskigamizige-Giizis**

May(Flower Budding Moon)- **Zaagibagaa-Giizis**

June(Strawberry Moon)- **Ode' imini-Giizis**

July(Half -Way, Summer Moon)- **Abitaa-Niibini-Giizis**

August(Wild Rice Moon)- **Manoominike-Giizis**

September(Leaves Changing Color Moon)- **Waatebagaa-Giizis**

October(Leaves Falling Moon)- **Binaakwe-Giizis**

November(Freezing Over Moon)- **Gashkadino-Giizis**

December(Little Spirit Moon)- **Manidoo-Giizisoons**

DAYS OF THE WEEK

Monday(day after prayer day)- **Ishwaa-anami'e giizhigad**

Tuesday(second day)- **Niizho-giizhigad**

Wednesday(half way)- **Aabitoose**

Thursday(fourth day)- **Niiyo giizhigad**

Friday(fifth day)- **Naano giizhigad**

Saturday(floor washing day)- **Giziibiigiisaginige-giizhigad**

Sunday(prayer day)- **Anami'e-giizhigad**

BODY PARTS

Arm(s)- **Ninik(an)**

Back(s)- **Nipikwan(an)**

Ear(s)- **Nitawag(an)**

Eye(s)- **Nishkiinzhig(oon)**

Finger(s)- **Nininjiins(an)**

Foot(feet)- **Ninzid(an)**

Head(s)- **Nishtigwaan(an)**

Heart(s)- **Ninde'(an)**

Hand(s)- **Ninij(iin)**

Leg(s)- **Nikaad(an)**

Mouth(s)- **Nindoon(an)**

Nose(s)- **Injaanzh(an)**

Stomach(s)- **Nimsad(an)**

Toe(s)- **Niibinaakwaanizidaan(an)**

Tongue(s)- **Nindenaniw(an)**

OTHER

Birch bark- **Wiigwaas**

Blanket(s)-

Waabooyaan(an)

Casino-**Endazhi-ataading**

College(s)-

Gabe-gikendaasoowigamig

Dancers- **Naamiwaad**

Day- **Giizhigad**

Drink- **Minikwe**

Drum(s)- **Dewe'igan(ag)**

Earth- **Aki**

Eat- **Wiisini**

Feather(s)- **Miigwan(ag)**

Gas Station- **Waasamoobimide-adaawewigamig**

Hospital- **Aakoziiwigamig**

Lake(s)- **Zaaga'igan(an)**

Medicine Man- **Mashkikiiwinini**

Medicine Woman- **Mashkikiikwe**

Money- **Zhooniyaa**

Moon(s)- **Dibiki-giizis(oog)**

Night- **Dibikad**

No- **Gaawiin**

Ojibwe people(s)- **Anishinaabe(g)**

Ojibwe language- **Anishinaabemowin**

Outside- **Agwajiing**

Pipe(s)- **Opwaagan(ag)**

Powwow- **Niimi'idim**

Restaurant- **Wiisiniiwigamig**

River(s)- **Ziibi(wan)**

School- **Gikinoo'amaadiiwigamig**

Singers- **Negamowaad**

Smudge-**Nookwezigan**

Star(s)- **Anang(oog)**

Store- **Adaawewigamig**

Stream(s)- **Ziibiins(an)**

Sun- **Giizis**

Sunset- **Bangishimog**

Today(now)- **Noongom**

Tonight- **Noongom dibikad**

Town(s)- **Oodena(wan)**

Warrior(s)- **Ogichidaa(wag)**

Yes- **Eya'**

28

RESERVATIONS:

Bad River- **Mashkii-ziibing**

Bay Mills- **Gnoozhekaaning**

Fond du Lac- **Nagaajiwanaang**

Grand Portage- **Gichi-Oniigaming**

Keewenaw Bay- **Wiikwedong**

Lac Courte Oreilles- **Odaawaa-zaaga'iganiing**

Lac du Flambeau- **Waaswaaganing**

Lac Vieux Desert- **Getegitigaaning**

Leech Lake- **Gaa-Zagaskwaajimekaag**

MilleLacs Lake- **Misi-Zaaga'iganing**

Nett Lake- **Asabiikone-Zaaga'iganing**

Red Cliff- **Gaa-Miskwaabikaag**

Red Lake- **Miskwaagamiiwi-Zaaga'iganing**

Mole Lake- **Zaka'aaganing**

Sault Ste Marie- **Baawitigong**

Vermilion Lake- **Onamani-Zaaga'iganing**

White Earth- **Gaa-Waabaabiganikaag**

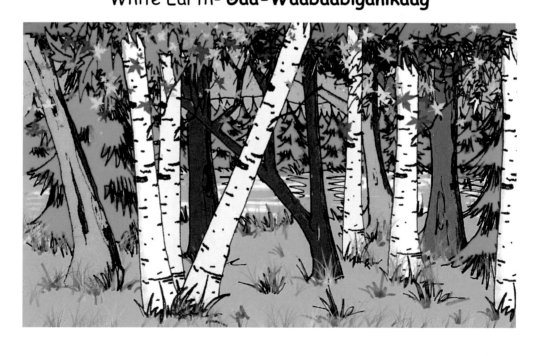

Manufactured by Amazon.ca
Bolton, ON

16104658R00019